Reading Readiness Songs

Singing Across the Curriculum

by Sara Jordan

Produced and Published by
Sara Jordan Publishing

a division of

℗© MCMXCII Jordan Music Productions Inc.
(SOCAN)

ISBN 1 - 895523 - 09 - 5

Credits

Producer, Composer, Lyricist - Sara Jordan
Digital Illustration Assistant - Ishrat Rahim
Female Singer and Rapper - Gail Selkirk
Male Singer and Rapper - Eric Maher
Male Singer (Consonant Song) - Blaine Selkirk
Narration (Months, Seasons, Days of the Week) - Sara Jordan
Children Singers - Benjamin and Jessica Jordan-Brough
Recording Engineer - Mark Shannon, Sound Image Productions
Layout and Cover Design - Campbell Creative Services
    and Darryl Taylor

For further information contact:

Jordan Music Productions Inc.
M.P.O. Box 490
Niagara Falls, NY
U.S.A. 14302-0490

Jordan Music Productions Inc.
Station M, Box 160
Toronto, Ontario
Canada, M6S 4T3

Internet: http://www.sara-jordan.com
e-mail: sjordan@sara-jordan.com
Telephone: 1-800-567-7733

℗© MCMXCII Sara Jordan Publishing and
Jordan Music Productions Inc. (SOCAN)
All rights reserved.

For the purposes of individual or institutions located in the United States, permission is given to reproduce one set for your classroom purposes.

In territories other than the United States, reproduction of the whole or any part of this publication is permitted only with the express written permission of the copyright holder, or under a licence from Access Copyright, The Canadian Copyright Licensing Agency or another national reprographic rights organization.

*Dedicated to my music teachers
who gave me so much more than lessons
for so many years.*

Table of Contents

Hints for Teachers and Parents 6

1. Funky Phonics 8

2. The Vowel Song 10

3. Consonants (C and G / multicultural theme) . . . 14
   Exercise 17

4. The Animal Song (Alphabet) 18
   Crossword Puzzle 25

5. Days of the Week 26

6. Who's Going to Save Us Now? 29
   (Continents and Oceans/Environment)

7. Telling Time 32

8. Android (Time and How We Spend It) 36

9. Coupons (Money and Environment) 38
   Exercise 41

10. The Months 42

11. The Seasons 44

Hints for Teachers and Parents

*T*here are many different schools of thought among educators and parents about exactly how children and adults learn to read. Frank Smith, in his book, *Insult to Intelligence*, outlines how students do *not* become thinking individuals through mindless hours of rote learning, and that students learn when we least expect it.

Rudolph Flesch however, author of the famous book *Why Johnny Can't Read*, totally supports the phonics approach, and blames the popular "look and say" method as the reason for the high illiteracy rate we still experience across North America.

Most teachers try not to rely *totally* on the drill method of phonics, the "look and say" method, flashcards, or rote memory work.

The *Reading Readiness Songs* audio kit, addresses the problems of today's beginning reader by creating a series of songs that use *both* context along with simple decoding strategies (i.e. decoding letter sounds of consonants at the beginning of words) to allow students to experience early reading success.

Being able to discriminate between sounds auditorily is indispensable to phonics instruction. By listening to rhyming songs and following along in the lyrics book, readers learn to read using auditory discrimination, decoding clues, as well as the "look and say" method.

Topics such as telling time, days of the week, months of the year, money, seasons, animals, the alphabet, multiculturalism and the environment are used, giving this resource a place across the curriculum.

In this way, reading does not become something that is studied during a certain block of time each day, but something that is carried over into many areas of study, from music to science, from math to telling time.

Most will agree, that the problem facing our young, is not so much one of illiteracy, but aliteracy (their choosing not to read). In a fast-paced society where we are bombarded with television, videos, music, and arcade games, *Reading Readiness Songs* approaches reading through songs with melodies and lyrics so compelling, that they're hard to put down.

A few ways to use this resource:

Within the class

- ✓ *Reading Readiness Songs* can be used to introduce many different units of study. Students tend to memorize factual information (i.e. names of months of the year etc.), when they are presented in the rhyme of a song.
- ✓ *Reading Readiness Songs* works well in independent learning centers with headphones and as a remedial tutor for students.

At Home

- ✓ Whether your child listens on the family stereo, through a stereo headset, or in the car as you run errands, you'll notice that reading will become simple and a pleasure for your child, when he/she chooses to read through the lyrics.

Nº 1

Funky Phonics

chorus twice:

F... F... PH...
Funky Phonics

F... F... PH...
Funky Phonics

F... F... PH...
Funky Phonics

Funky...
Funky...

Reading's not rough.
Learning's not tough.
We can't get enough ... of
Funky Phonics.

Just off the cuff.
We love this stuff.
More than mere fluff ... it's
Funky Phonics.

chorus twice:

Reading Readiness Songs © MCMXCII Sara Jordan Publishing

Now Funky Phonics is
Really neat.
It's the finest thing.
It can't be beat.

This first in the series
Will make you aware.
Of global issues we deal with
Out there.

We'll learn the days,
Seasons and time.
And about pollution
And why it's a crime.

We'll sing and we'll dance
And we'll learn how to read.
'Cause Funky Phonics
Is all we need!!

chorus twice:

Nº 2

Vowel Song
(long and short sounds)

chorus:

A, E, I, O, U...
Sometimes Y's
a vowel too.

A, E, I, O, U...
Sometimes Y's
a vowel too.

A, E, I, O, U...
Sometimes Y's
a vowel too.

A, E, I, O, U...
Sometimes Y's
a vowel too.

Just as we build
   homes with windows,
We use vowels to
   build words too;
Vowel sounds
   can be long or short sounds,
We've got a vowel rap
   song for you.

There are a few general rules
For vowels and their sounds;
So listen up! Pay attention!
Here are some that've been around.

When a word ends with silent 'e'
Or two vowels walk along,
The first vowel's long and says its name.
You'll hear this in our song.

chorus:

Mat + e = mate.

Fat + e = fate.

Bat (squeeze in i) = bait.

Pant (squeeze in i) = paint.

Rid + e = ride.

Hid + e = hide.

Did (squeeze in e) = died.

Lid (squeeze in e) = lied.

chorus:

Sometimes we say vowels with short sounds,
If they're found inside short words;
Listen up! and Listen closely!
Here are a few short vowels we've heard.

"a" sounds like

at
cat   and
mat

mad
sad   and
fad.

"e" as in

get
set   and
yet

net
pet   and
let

"i" as in

in
bin and
win

fin
tin and
sin

"o" as in

job
rob and
Bob

and "u" as in

scrub and
tub

chorus:

N° 3

Consonants
(hard and soft C and G)

chorus:

The kids in our neighborhood
Play together, like kids should.
If only our world's countries could
Be like us in our neighborhood.

The letters in our alphabet
Form words together, better yet,
The sounds they make
    often depend
On neighboring letters,
    and how they blend.

The kids I play with on the street
Know many different games;
Their families come from 'round the world
But basically kids are all the same.

Some letters in our alphabet
Have several different sounds.
They help to make our language rich.
We're glad that they are all around.

chorus:

Take for example the letter "c"
Sometimes it sounds like "k".
We get this /k/ /k/ sound of "c".
When it's followed by an "o" or "a".

But sometimes "c" can sound like "s"
When its followed by "e" or "i".
Why don't I sing a song about kids.
With /k/ and /s/ ? - Here I'll try.

Caribbean kids bring to my street,
Calypso, I crave that beat.
At Caribana we "jump up" in the heat,
Calypso at Caribana's Carnival's neat.

Our cities never cease to be
Centers for certain ceremonies.
Some have become civic holidays.
They all have importance, in many ways.

So now you know the sounds of "C".
But how are you at sounds of "G"?
When "G" is followed by "i" or "e",
We say /j/ for letter "G."

When "G" is followed by "o", "a" or "u",
It gives the /g/ sound like in ..."guru".
So right now, I'll sing for you,
A song with the /g/ and /j/ sound too.

*My good friend Gavin's Guyanese,
His great grandma cooks to please;
Gilbacker, goat and some peas,
I love good food that's Guyanese.*

*Coming from the German club,
Aroma of sausage and sauerkraut;
Generally what I like the best,
Is how Germans celebrate Oktoberfest.*

*The kids in our neighborhood
Play together, like kids should.
If only our world's countries could
Be like us in our neighborhood.*

Exercise

Fill in the blanks to complete the hard "c" and soft "c" words that you see in each picture.

c __ m __ __

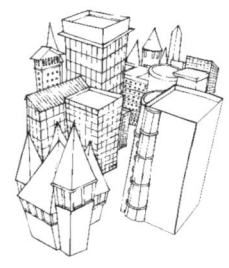

c __ t __

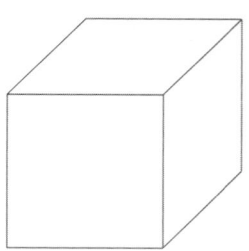

c __ __ e

c __ __ t

c a __ __

c __ r e __ __

N° 4

The Animal Song
(The Alphabet)

A   B   C   D   E   F   G
H   I   J   K   L   M   N   O   P
Q   R   S   T   U   V
W   X   Y   Zed or Zee.
    - again-

chorus 2x:

    Funk it up,
    Funk it up,
    With the Animal Song;
    With the Animal Song;
    With so many different kinds,
    With so many different kinds,
    We could sing all day long.
    We could sing all day long.

A's for Amoeba,
A single-celled creature
Reproduces by "fission",
Among things.

B is for **B**at,
The only mammal that
Flies through the sky
With webbed wings.

C is for **C**at,
And just like a bat
It cleans itself with
Its pink tongue.

D's for **D**og,
My friend when I jog.
The Animal Song's
Just begun.

chorus 2x:

E is for **E**lephant,
Its long trunk so elegant;
But really it's just
A long nose.

F is for **F**ish,
The kind that goes swish
Its fins help it swim
As it goes.

G is for **G**oat,
With its horns and warm coat
And a beard
That makes it look wise.

H is for **H**orse,
That runs fast of course.
Its single-toed foot's
No surprise.

chorus 2x:

I's for **I**guana,
A lizardly fauna,
Eating fruits, leaves
And plants.

J's fo **J**ellyfish,
We try not to squish,
Walking barefoot
In the sand.

K's for **K**angaroo,
With hind limbs it uses
To leap
Wherever it goes.

L is for **L**ion,
With its long mane it's tryin'
To find food pacing
To and fro.

chorus 2x:

M's for the **M**oles,
That burrow long holes
45 feet
In an hour.

N is for **N**ewt.
Some are red some are cute.
Both water and air
Give them power.

O's for **O**possum.
This mammal's awesome.
Gestation takes only
12 days.

P is for **P**orcupine,
With its prickly spine;
Protecting itself
In this way.

chorus 2x:

Q is for **Q**uail.
Some say it looks frail.
This ground living bird
Likes tall grass.

R's for Raccoon.
In the light of the moon,
It looks like a thief
With its mask.

S for Sand Dollar,
That lives in deep water.
With a five star design
On its shell.

T is for Turtle,
With its armor shell girdle.
It likes being
In water as well.

chorus 2x:

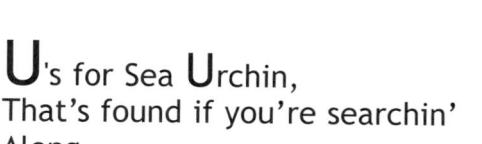

U's for Sea Urchin,
That's found if you're searchin'
Along
The bed of the sea.

V is for **V**ulture.
In this bird's culture
They often will feast
On dead meat.

W's for **W**allaby,
A small kangaroo you see

And **X** is for o**X**,
Both run free.

Y is for **Y**ak,
Cold it can hack.

Z's Zebra,
Some also say Z.

chorus 2x:

A   B   C   D   E   F   G
H   I   J   K   L   M   N   O   P
Q   R   S   T   U   V
W   X   Y   Zed or Zee.
    - again-

Exercise

Complete the crossword below.

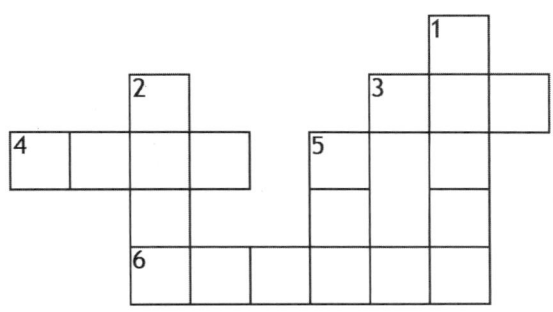

Across   Down

Nº 5

Days of the Week

chorus:

S S ... S for Sunday

M M ... M for Monday

T T ... T for Tuesday

Rappin' the days of the week is cool.

W W ... W for Wednesday

Th Th ... Th for Thursday

F F ... F for Friday

S for Saturday. I'm no fool!

S is for Sunday.
It's named for the sun.
It's Day Number One.
Our week has begun.

M is for Monday,
Named after the moon.
More days named for planets
Will follow soon.

T is for Tuesday,
For the war god, Tiw.
Tiw's another word for Mars
Which we use in lieu.

chorus:

W's for Wednesday,
For planet Mercury.
It came from the name Woden's day.
It's easy, you can see.

Th is for Thursday,
For the god Thor;
Another name for Jupiter.
We've got two more.

chorus:

F is for Friday,
For Frigg's the goddess of love.
The planet for Frigg
Is Venus above.

S is for Saturday,
For Saturn in the sky.
So, you see, man's named the days
For planets way up high.

chorus:

N° 6

Who's Going to Save Us Now?

(Continents, Oceans and the Environment)

chorus 2x:

Who's going to save us now?
Who's going to save us now?
Who's going to save us now?
Some way? Some how?

I lived on this land
Many years ago.
When wildlife was safe
And plants could freely grow.

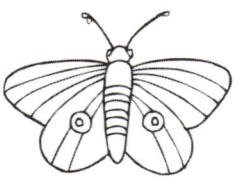

Each time I return
I must hold back my tears
And wonder what we've undone
To earth in recent years.

chorus 2x:

Man's one of a million
Species that share this earth,
But only man can undo
The mess that's caused this dearth.

Our countries have set out
In our interest to protect
Endangered species and spaces
Lest we forget.

chorus 2x:

Our seven continents
Can really show they care,
Or oceans between us
Will become seas of despair.

Asia and Africa,
And Australia ... through
Europe, North and South America
Antartica too.

chorus 2x:

Because of pollutants
Our oceans are crying.
Because of man's destruction
Our oceans are dying.

The Pacific, Atlantic
The Indian and Arctic,
Ocean life, suffers too
With every oil slick.

chorus 2x:

N° 7

Telling Time

5, 10, 15, 20, 25, 30, 35, 40

45, 50, 55, 60...
Telling time is really nifty.

8 o'clock
I rise from bed.
Do my teeth
After I'm fed.

At 8:15
I bike to school.
Ride with care,
Not like a fool.

8:30 now
Or half past eight.
Can't afford
To be there late.

8:45
The school bell rings.
Lockers slam
As kids grab things.

5, 10, 15, 20, 25, 30, 35, 40

45, 50, 55, 60...
Telling time is really nifty.

It's 9 o'clock,
Classes start.
We like school.
It makes us smart.

9:05
The anthem plays.
That's how we start
Each single day.

9:10 now,
The teacher speaks
And tells us what
We'll do this week.

9:15 or
Quarter past.
We learn so much.
We learn so fast.

5, 10, 15, 20, 25, 30, 35, 40

45, 50, 55, 60...
Telling time is really nifty.

9:20 now,
The minutes pass.
It's so much fun
In our class.

9:25
I choose my book.
I like just how
The pictures look.

9:30 now,
Or half past nine.
So far my day
Has been just fine.

9:35
Is sometimes said
"It's 25 to 10"
Instead.

5, 10, 15, 20, 25, 30, 35, 40

45, 50, 55, 60...
Telling time is really nifty.

9:40 ... the
Big hand's at 8.
One tardy kid
Has walked in late.

9:45 ... or
Quarter to 10;
I glance at the clock
Now and then.

9:50 now
Or 10 to 10;
One famous clock
Is called Big Ben.

9:55

And then it's 10,
When a new hour
Starts again.

5, 10, 15, 20, 25, 30, 35, 40

45, 50, 55, 60...

Reading Readiness Songs © MCMXCII Sara Jordan Publishing

Nº 8

Android
(Seconds, Minutes, Hours)

Rustle, rustle, hustle, bustle,
Android is my name.
Rustle, hustle, bustle,
Ac-quis-i-tion is my game.

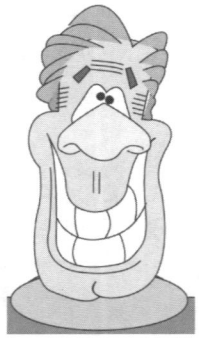

60 seconds in a minute;
60 minutes in an hour.
Time is scarce.
Time is precious.
Time is money.
Time is power.

24 hours in a day,
I work them all;
It's just my way.
24 hours in a day,
He works them all;
That's just his way.

I chisel here and chisel there,
Scraping profits everywhere.
I feel like someone going somewhere.
Android is my name.

24 hours in a day,
No time for laughter, none for play.
24 hours in a day,
No time for laughter, none for play.

Nº 9

Coupons
(Money, Environment)

Sing twice:
Clip your coupons!
Save your money!
This recession
Isn't funny.
Clip your coupons!

*We've had enough!
Let's cut out
This 'coupon stuff'!*

Wise consumers
Can save pennies,
Nickels, dimes and
Quarters too.

Coupons waste
Our time and forests.
That's no good
For me and you.

So the next time that I go shopping
Where they have this coupon jive,
I'll just look at them and holler,
"Keep our minds and trees alive."

Sing twice:
Clip your coupons!
Save your money!
This recession
Isn't funny.
Clip your coupons!

We've had enough!
Let's cut out
This 'coupon stuff'!

Save 5 cents, that's a nickel.
Save 10 cents, that's a dime.
Save 25 you'll save a quarter.
See I know my money fine.

100 cents make a dollar.
In America it's a dollar bill.

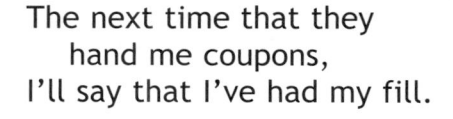

The next time that they
   hand me coupons,
I'll say that I've had my fill.

Keep your coupons!
Keep your money!
Mindless waste
Isn't funny.

Keep your coupons!
Save WHAT we've got!
We'll use our heads.
And save a lot.

Keep your coupons!
Keep your money!
Mindless waste
Isn't funny.

Keep your coupons!
Save WHAT we've got!
We'll use our heads.
And save a lot.

Exercise

Draw lines to connect each country to the currency it uses.

Hint: You may need to use the internet or an encyclopedia to find the answers.

Country	Currency
USA	Peso
Russia	Rand
United Kingdom	Ruble
Mexico	Rupee
Japan	Dollar
South Africa	Pound Sterling
India	Yen

N° 10

The Months

chorus twice:

January, February,
March, April,
May, June and July,

August, September, October,
November, December,
Months are easy to remember!

The time earth takes
    to circle the sun
Is 365 days.
When the circle's complete,
    a new year's begun.
Man counts years in this way.

The length of our month
    Is loosely based too
On the orbit 'round earth
    of the moon.
But if each of our months
    were 29 1/2 days,
We'd end our year too soon.

chorus twice:

The idea of monthly calendars
    is very, very old;
Sumerians devised the first
    5,000 years ago.
Pope Gregory the XIII
    In 1582
Made final calendar changes
    used today by me and you.

chorus twice:

Nº 11

The Seasons

chorus twice:

Winter and spring,
Summer and fall;
These are the seasons.
We love them all.

As earth rotates once a day,
Daytime turns to night,
'Cause when we slowly
 turn on earth
The sun goes out of sight.

Earth also revolves once a year,
Circling the sun.
How earth tilts while travelling round,
Makes seasons go and come.

chorus twice:

When the northern half or
 hemisphere
Tilts towards the sun,
The earth begins to warm up,
And soon spring has begun.

At the same time, in the southern half,
The southern hemisphere,
The earth begins to cool down;
They say that "autumn's here."

chorus twice:

The thing that makes summers warm
Or brings on winter's cold,
Is the miracle of our earth's path.
It's worth its weight in gold.

Our planet's path takes one whole year,
And then it starts again;
As we watch in awe the changes
And greet each new season.

chorus twice:

Ask your retailer about other excellent audio programs by teacher, Sara Jordan

Funky Phonics®: Learn to Read Volumes 1-4

Blending the best in educational research and practice, Sara Jordan's four part series provides students with the strategies needed to decode words through rhyming, blending and segmenting. Teachers and parents love the lessons and activities while children will find the catchy, toe-tapping tunes fun.
IN ENGLISH

Songs and Activities for Early Learners™

Dynamic songs teach the alphabet, counting, parts of the body, members of the family, colors, shapes, fruit and more. Helps students of all ages to learn basic vocabulary easily. The kit includes a lyrics book with activities teachers may reproduce for their classes.
IN ENGLISH, FRENCH OR SPANISH

Thematic Songs for Learning Language™

Delightful collection of songs and activities teaching salutations, rooms of the house, pets, meals, food and silverware, transportation, communication, parts of the body, clothing, weather and prepositions. (Great for ESL classes.) The kit includes a lyrics book with activities teachers may reproduce for their classes. IN ENGLISH, FRENCH OR SPANISH

Reading Readiness Songs

This great introduction to reading uses both phonics and whole language approaches. Topics covered include the alphabet, vowels, consonants, telling time, days of the week, seasons, the environment and more! Accompanying lyrics book includes helpful hints for parents and teachers.
VERSIONS IN ENGLISH, FRENCH OR SPANISH

Grammar Grooves vol.1™

Ten songs that teach about nouns, pronouns, adjectives, verbs, tenses, adverbs and punctuation. Activities and puzzles, which may be reproduced, are included in the lyrics book to help reinforce learning even further. A complement of music tracks to the ten songs is included for karaoke performances. Also great for music night productions.
IN ENGLISH, FRENCH OR SPANISH

Lullabies Around the World
*** Parents' Choice Award Winner! ***
*** Directors' Choice Award Winner! ***
Traditional lullabies sung by native singers with translated verses in English. Multicultural activities are included in the lyrics book. Includes a complement of music tracks for class performances.
Pre-K - Grade 3   IN 11 DIFFERENT LANGUAGES

Healthy Habits™
*** Directors' Choice Award Winner! ***
Songs and activities covering nutrition, the food pyramid, anatomy, dental hygiene, personal and fire safety. The lyrics book which accompanies the recording has activities which can be reproduced for the class. A complement of music accompaniment tracks works well for performances.
Pre-K - Grade 3   IN ENGLISH

The Presidents' Rap®
The legends of the American Presidents live on in classical, swing, dixie, pop and rap music. A musical treasure trove of tid-bits of information about each President. Very popular among teachers wanting to put on musical shows in their schools. IN ENGLISH

The Math Unplugged™ Series
Available for Addition, Subtraction, Division and Multiplication. Tuneful songs teach kids the basic math facts. Repetitive, musical and fun. A great resource. Each audio kit includes a lyrics book with worksheet pages which may be reproduced.
IN ENGLISH

Celebrate the Human Race™
*** Directors' Choice Award Winner! ***
Learn about The Seven Natural Wonders of the World and the children who live in those places. Music is representative of each country or place studied. The kit includes a lyrics book with activities which teachers may reproduce for their classes.
IN ENGLISH

Celebrate Seasons™

A delightful collection of songs and activities about fall and deciduous trees, migration and hibernation, how animals prepare for winter, spring and maple syrup, flowers and pollination, solstices and equinoxes and how seasons differ in other parts of the world. The lyrics book includes related activities which teachers are free to reproduce for classroom use. A complement of instrumental versions of the ten songs makes class performances a breeze! IN ENGLISH

Celebrate Holidays™

An inspiring collection of songs and activities teaching about Halloween, Thanksgiving, Chanukah, Christmas, New Year's celebrations, Valentine's Day, St. Patrick's Day and Easter plus a patriotic national birthday song. The lyrics book includes over a dozen activity sheets. A complement of ten instrumental tracks allows students to become "performers", boosting literacy skills and making "performances" a lot of fun.
IN ENGLISH

Bilingual Songs™ Volumes 1-4
NEW Bilingual Preschool

*** Parents' Choice Award Winner! ***

The perfect way to have fun while acquiring a second language. This series teaches the basic alphabet, counting to 100, days of the week, months of the year, colors, food, animals, parts of the body, clothing, family members, emotions, places in the community and the countryside, measurement, opposites, greetings, gender, articles, plural forms of nouns, adjectives, pronouns, adverbs of frequency, question words and much more!
ENGLISH–SPANISH and ENGLISH–FRENCH

NEW Resource and Activity Books

We have developed a series of reproducible resource/activity books to be used as supplemental learning aids. Please visit our website to view these titles online.

Please visit our website, www.SongsThatTeach.com, for free educational games, songs, activities and more.

For help finding a retailer near you contact
Sara Jordan Publishing 1-800-567-7733